What Should I Know about my Child's SELF-ESTEEM?

Germain Duclos

What Should I Know about my Child's SELF-ESTEEM?

Éditions du
CHU Sainte-Justine

Bibliothèque et Archives nationales du Québec and Library and Archives Canada cataloguing in publication

Duclos, Germain
What should I know about my child's self-esteem?
(Questions/answers for parents)
Translation of: Que savoir sur l'estime de soi de mon enfant?.

ISBN 978-2-89619-143-7

1. Self-esteem in children - Miscellanea. 2. Child psychology - Miscellanea. 3. Parent and child - Miscellanea. I. Title.

BF723.S3D82613 2008 155.4'182 C2008-942290-2

Cover design: Quatuor
Graphic Design: Nicole Tétreault
Cover page photo: Claude Dolbec
Inside photos: Nancy Lessard

Éditions du CHU Sainte-Justine
3175, Côte-Sainte-Catherine
Montreal (Quebec) H3T 1C5
Telephone: (514) 345-4671 • Fax: (514) 345-4631
www.chu-sainte-justine.org/editions

ISBN: 978-2-89619-143-7

Legal Deposit: Bibliothèque et Archives nationales du Québec, 2008
Library and Archives Canada, 2008

The Sainte-Justine Hospital Foundation wishes to thank the generous donors who contributed to *UniverSanté des familles* and made it possible to create this new collection for families.

Thank you for your support... for the love of children!

Table of Contents

Definition and characteristics of self-esteem

Fostering a sense of security and confidence

Fostering a sense of competency

Being a competent parent

Definition and characteristics of self-esteem

Is self-esteem important?

Everyone needs to feel they possess an intrinsic value, independent from how they look, what they own, and how they perform in life. Each person intuitively perceives the importance of self-esteem; to be happy, you have to feel you are worth something. People need to find themselves acceptable. Feeling worthless means that life has no meaning.

Therefore everyone forms an image of himself or herself that varies considerably over time and experience. And in fact, this "self-portrait" continues to change for our entire lives, even at the age of 80.

When and how does self-esteem develop?

Fostering self-esteem essentially consists of accompanying and guiding children and teenagers in all aspects of their lives, emotional, social, intellectual and moral. The first years are of prime importance; they are the ones in which, in some sense, the human psyche is formed.

Numerous studies show that the period of early bonding with parents is fundamental in children's psychic development. It forms the very basis of self-esteem. This early feeling of self-worth is later enriched by the reactions of other people who highlight children's strengths, personal qualities and successes.

Finally, let us note that all children feel valued if they have quality relationships with the people who are important to them. No one is born with a ready-made self-image. Children first learn to see themselves in the eyes of people they consider important: parents, brothers and sisters, teachers as well as playmates.

Self-esteem develops according to a process that must be reinforced through concrete means, and most of all, by the appropriate educational attitudes. That is, when parents and educators display a warm attitude towards children, when they make themselves entirely available and provide them with the necessary attention, when they regularly emphasize the things children do well, when they believe in their ability to meet challenges, and when they avoid hurtful words and sarcasm.

What is a more precise definition of self-esteem?

Dictionaries generally define self-esteem as a positive feeling that comes from having a good sense of one's own value. Self-esteem is also described as the value a person places upon himself or herself as a whole; it is based on people's confidence in their own self-worth.

From my point of view, the most complete and finely detailed definition of self-esteem is that of Josianne de Saint-Paul:

Did you know?

Enjoyment of play, enjoyment of learning, enjoyment of living with other people, all these forms of enjoyment are important in the building of self-esteem.

"Self-esteem is the positive evaluation of oneself based on the awareness of one's worth and inalienable importance as a human being. People who value themselves, treat themselves with benevolence and feel worthy of love and happiness. Self-esteem is also based on a feeling of security that comes into being when we are sure of our ability to exercise our free will, special skills and faculty of learning to confront the events and challenges of life, responsibly and efficiently."

Thus, self-esteem is above all a positive judgment that a person makes about himself or herself, an awareness of personal worth in different areas of life. It is, in a sense, a set of attitudes and beliefs that help us face reality and the world in general.

How do children work towards self-esteem?

What can we do to develop children's self-esteem? First, babies discover their bodies in the warmth of their relationship with their parents, then with other people who take care of them with kisses and tender attentions. Protected, fed and caressed, children enjoy a sense of well-being inside their own skin.

Around 18 months, children enter a new period of their lives: they move, they get into things, they run around, but from this point onwards, they also want to decide, choose, assert themselves. Between 2 and 3 years, with the appearance of coherent language, children start to claim their independence. Their self-esteem depends on their parents' ability to recognize them as individuals who are different from themselves.

And so they continue to grow. Around 3 or 4, fears start to appear, as well as different strategies of manipulation and seduction. Children start to want to be closer to the opposite-sex parent. During this period, when children have not yet reached the stage of logical thought processes, they seek recognition and encouragement.

To "esteem" implies making a judgment, a function that requires a certain intellectual maturity. Thus it is with the emergence of logical thought processes, when children reach 7 or 8 years old, that self-esteem appears. Starting from this age, when children become capable of critical thought about themselves, they can evaluate their personal worth in all areas of their lives (relationships with their parents and friends, at school...), according to personal criteria or those of the people they consider important. This is when children start to evaluate themselves and also express esteem for others, through acts, words and attitudes.

Did you know?

Parents and educators must absolutely recognize the necessity of developing self-esteem. As research demonstrates, it is a key factor in preventing many problems common among young people: dropping out of school, learning difficulties, delinquency, drug and alcohol abuse, suicide.

When children start school, they move into a new phase. New mental structures incite them to make logical and practical judgments, to understand the rules of games, to cooperate within a group, and to want to learn new things. School age is also an age when the physical and social self-images are enriched by the intellectual self-image. Meanwhile, more and more people are making judgments about them (parents, friends, teachers and educators of all kinds). Words can be wounding; in the long run, they can even kill the inner "good Jonathan" or the inner "good Sophie". Violent gestures and negligence also do tremendous harm to children's self-esteem.

Perhaps the most important time for consolidating self-esteem is adolescence. Teens experience great vulnerability due to physical changes, mood swings, the need to distance themselves from parents and forge their own identities. However, in spite of sometimes difficult encounters, teenagers do not need our overprotection but instead, our recognition of their worth and reinforcement of their sense of pride.

Does the quality of children's relationships with adults affect their self-esteem ?

Self-esteem is greatly dependent on the quality of the relationships that children forge with the "significant" people in their lives, the people they consider important. If "important" adults have positive things to say about them, it greatly contributes to children's self-esteem. On the other hand, negative comments or judgments can destroy their image of themselves. It is clear that emotional attachment is a double-edged sword.

The more important an adult is to a child, the greater the repercussions of the comments the adult makes, positive or negative. Indeed, the quality of interpersonal exchange greatly influences self-esteem, that little flame that lights up children's eyes when they are proud of themselves but starts to flicker, and even becomes extinguished if exposed to sarcasm and criticism!

Children do not automatically develop healthy self-esteem because they experience small successes. It takes more than that for them to see themselves in a positive light. That is where adults come into the picture. Their role is to emphasize children's achievements and positive behaviours so that the children can remember them. Without this kind of constructive feedback, children cannot become aware of their successes nor record them in their memories. Adults must regularly go back and revive the memory of these accomplishments. Self-esteem thrives on memory.

Thus, self-esteem is closely linked to the relationships people have with themselves and others. The value we give ourselves is not independent from our esteem for the people around us. Children need their self-esteem to be confirmed by people who are important to them: parents, friends, educators and all significant adults.

How do children become aware of their own value?

Children's self-esteem depends first of all on the positive reactions of people who are important to them. These people, by emphasizing children's successes, confirm their sense of self-worth. Self-esteem comes first of all from external, or extrinsic sources.

In the development of self-esteem, what is most important is not that a child does something positive, but that he is told he has done so; for example: "You shared your toys with your friend", or "You helped Daddy set the table." It is important for parents to emphasize children's positive actions by showing that they are proud of them. This kind of feedback helps make children conscious that they have done something positive. Without these reactions, children would not achieve this awareness. Self-esteem is built on a process of growing awareness that is fostered by positive verbal reinforcement. Words reassure children and give them hope.

By receiving positive feedback on a regular basis, children gradually internalize healthy self-esteem; that esteem is based on an inner monologue, that is, a conversation they carry on with themselves in their heads which is positive in content.

What are the components of healthy self-esteem?

Self-esteem is made up of four components: feelings of security and confidence, self-knowledge, a sense of belonging to a group, and a sense of competency.

A sense of security and confidence is a prerequisite for self-esteem. People must first feel confident before they can learn what their self-esteem needs in order to flourish. The three other components are different. Self-knowledge, the sense of belonging and competency can be stimulated through the use of appropriate educational attitudes and sound methods at each stage of development and every period of life.

What attitudes and skills are possessed by children with a positive self-image?

Children who have a positive view of themselves adopt the following attitudes and skills:

- security and relaxation;
- a general sense of well-being;
- a feeling of confidence around adults;
- the ability to remember their successes;
- the ability to perceive their own qualities and skills;
- a sense of confidence in their own abilities;
- the ability to confront new events;
- the motivation to learn and confront new challenges;
- perseverance in the face of difficulty;
- the ability to perceive their differences;
- the ability to perceive and accept the differences of others;
- the ability to inspire the respect of others;
- self-assertiveness and independence;
- initiative;
- imagination and creative ability;
- the ability to peacefully resolve social conflicts;
- the ability to cooperate;
- a sense of well-being in a group.

Children cannot display all these attitudes and skills at once. However, if we foster their self-esteem, children will be more likely to incorporate these attitudes and skills into their lives.

Did you know?

Self-esteem is born in close and loving relationship. Anyone who has once felt loved or still feels loved – if only by one other person – can tell themselves that they are loveable and valuable.

What parental attitudes have a positive or negative bearing on self-esteem?

Positive attitudes	Negative attitudes
Be warm and available to children.	Fail to provide a stable psychological environment Fail to be physically present on a regular basis.
Be reliable in meeting children's needs.	Fail to respond to children's needs.
Express unconditional love.	Have unrealistic expectations . Show love only if children "perform" well.
Emphasize and praise children's important accomplishments	Ignore children's accomplishments or fail to consider them important.
Acknowledge children's difficulties, sparing their pride and providing means for improvement.	Blame children for shortcomings.
Provide a stable environment, in terms of space and time.	Fail to provide a stable lifestyle.
Establish rules of conduct that are reassuring and clear.	Fail to establish rules, or apply them inconsistently.
Be consistent in the application of rules.	Constantly change attitude when applying the rules of conduct.
Be firm on important issues, and flexible on others.	Be too strict or too permissive.

Positive attitudes	Negative attitudes
Reduce children's stress factors by preparing them for change, keeping changes to a minimum, and helping them find ways of calming down when stressed.	Show obvious signs of stress. Overestimate children's ability to adjust.
Be an adult who can be trusted.	Fail to demonstrate openness and availability.
Reactivate the memory of children's past accomplishments.	Ignore children's accomplishments or fail to acknowledge their importance.
Highlight children's strengths.	Emphasize children's difficulties rather than their strengths.
Support children in the face of difficulties.	Overprotect children.
Encourage children to find solutions to their problems.	Solve children's problems for them.
Use positive language that promotes their self-worth.	Use hurtful words. Humiliate children, use sarcasm.
Encourage children's expression of feelings and emotions.	Discourage children's expression of feelings and needs, or dismiss them.
Display openness to others.	Over-control children's social relationships.
Encourage acts of generosity and cooperation.	Instill individualism and competitiveness.

Positive attitudes	Negative attitudes
Encourage children to make friends and manage disputes on their own.	Resolve children's disputes for them.
Give children responsibilities that are appropriate for their level.	Have expectations that are too high or too low.
Encourage children to make their own choices and develop their independence.	Maintain children's dependence and exert excessive control.
Encourage children's creativity.	Ignore or fail to value children's creativity.
Encourage children's sense of initiative.	Ignore or fail to highlight children's initiative.
Respect children's own motivation.	Impose parents' motivations on children.
Respect children's own pace of development.	Focus solely on results.
Emphasize the learning process rather than results.	Focus solely on results.
Acknowledge that mistakes sometimes happen.	Impose adult perfectionism on children, and blame them for their mistakes.
De-dramatize mistakes.	Impose adult perfectionism on children.

Did you know?

Healthy self-esteem does not mean being nice, but rather, being aware of our strengths and limitations, and accepting what is most personal and precious in us. It also means taking on responsibilities, asserting ourselves, knowing how to respond to our own needs, having personal goals and acquiring the means for attaining them. Healthy self-esteem requires personal integrity and consideration for others.

Fostering a sense of security and confidence

What makes up a sense of security?

The need for security is great for adults, and even more fundamental for children. Out of all young mammals, human babies are the ones who depend most, and longest, on those around them, especially when it comes to physical and psychological security.

Children must first feel exogenous (or external) security, which progressively changes into endogenous (or internal) security, and with time transforms into an attitude of confidence in themselves and others.

Certain educational "basics" must be observed in order for children to have a sense of physical and psychological security. Above all, the educational environment (home, day-care, school) needs to be organized in such a way as to guarantee children's security.

At the physical level, parents must choose an educational environment (day-care, school) that provides adequate supervision. Moreover, educators and care-givers must eliminate, or place out of children's reach, anything that could prove dangerous (medicine, toxic products, stove dials, electrical outlets, etc.) and respect certain basic safety measures (adequate lighting in stairways, for example). Children must also be taught strategies and concrete ways of dealing with danger when no adult is present. Children must understand these rules of safety very clearly. When they realize that they are being protected against accidents or illness, they feel valued and important, which promotes their self-esteem.

Some parents attribute less importance to the question of psychological security. And yet this form of security is just as fundamental to children's development. With regular care and the consistent presence of the adults in their lives, children gradually attain a sense of psychological security and confidence about themselves and others.

What educational attitudes promote a sense of security?

A reassuring presence and attitude

Today, adults are often pulled in many directions at once, and have less and less time to devote to children. Children who do not receive a steady level of attention can suffer from emotional neglect and conclude that they are unworthy of their parents' time. It is essential for children to be given time and attention

Ensuring stability

Frequent changes in children's routines provoke instability and feelings of insecurity, which tends to lower their confidence level. Routines make children feel secure and give them stable landmarks in space and time. At times when changes are significant and frequent, parents must ensure the greatest possible stability for their children.

Developing self-discipline

It is essential for children to learn to distinguish permissible behaviours from those that are forbidden. Though it is sometimes difficult, they must learn to regulate and adapt their conduct to their surroundings. This self-discipline is gradually acquired from early childhood through adolescence.doit apprendre, et cela est parfois pénible, à réguler et à adapter ses conduites en fonction des réalités qui l'entourent. Cette autodiscipline s'acquiert graduellement, de la petite enfance à l'adolescence.

Reassuring rules of conduct

All environments need rules in order to function. At school and at home, adults must develop rules of conduct whose goal is to ensure the child's sense of security. By providing children with stable points of reference, adults help them adapt to their environment and embrace certain values.

The rules should have the following characteristics:

- They must be adapted to the **children's age** and take account of their **level of development** and **needs**.
- They must be **clear**, that is, they must reflect values that children can understand (respect of self and others, and the environment).
- They must be **concrete**, constructive and realistic.
- They must be **consistent**, that is, they must not vary according to the adult's mood. To help ensure consistency, rules should be limited in number.
- They must be **coherent**. Thus it is essential that adults "practice what they preach" in terms of the values they wish to transmit.

- They must be **logical**, for children must learn to face the consequences of their actions and words if we want them to internalize a sense of personal responsibility.

Acknowledgement of good behaviour

It is important to regularly emphasize children's good behaviour with some form of recognition or congratulations to make them aware of the value of their actions.

Helping children manage their stress

Children experience a great deal of stress when faced with changes and new things, which make them feel insecure. Thus it is important to help them manage this stress, while taking action to deal with the sources of their feelings of insecurity.

Where do feelings of confidence come from?

Feelings of confidence come from what is called external (outside) security and are reinforced in children when adults keep their promises. When this occurs, adults are perceived by children as trustworthy and reassuring. Children can then interiorize a feeling of confidence, which is what gives them hope in the future.

Did you know?

Stress is not completely negative. Stress can actually put our adaptation skills to work, help us overcome certain challenges and generally progress. Of course, it all depends on our way of dealing with it.

The feeling of having confidence in others progressively transforms into self-confidence. A sense of security and trust in significant adults enables children to venture out and explore their environment, for they know that someone is there to protect or help them if a danger arises.

To instill feelings of confidence in children, you must trust them. Parents and educators must believe in children's ability to adapt. It is their job to support children's initiatives, praise them for learning and protect without overprotecting them.

What are the signs that children feel confident and secure?

Children who feel secure and confident display most of the following attitudes and behaviours. They are:

- confident with adults they know;
- able to physically relax;
- able to accept physical contact;
- able to adapt to stress;
- able to remain calm when physically injured;
- able to remain calm when in physical discomfort;
- able to tolerate delays;
- able to look forward to enjoyment;
- able to react positively to new things;
- able to take calculated risks;
- able to form a mental image of time;
- able to be optimistic about the future;
- able to understand and accept the meaning of rules;
- able to respond positively to rules.

What are the parental attitudes that foster confidence in children?

- Ensure children's stability by maintaining a regular schedule; provide a stable environment, in terms of space and time.
- Establish set routines and rituals.
- Remain stable and dependable in responses to children's physical and emotional needs.
- Ensure children's physical safety by eliminating sources of physical danger and illness.
- Set aside time to play with children.
- Provide security and affection when children are ill or injured.

Did you know?

- Small children who feel reassured by their relationships with their parents are more independent, react better to separation and have greater self-esteem when they start school.
- It is not possible to develop a good self-image if one lives in a constant state of fear or worry. Everyone needs stability to build feelings of confidence about themselves and others. Parents can provide this stability by keeping changes to a minimum, setting realistic boundaries and responding to children's needs.

- Provide security and affection by being receptive to children's emotions: anger, sadness, fear, etc.
- Keep promises.
- Gauge an appropriate time-lapse between the expression and satisfaction of children's desires.
- Avoid excessive mood swings.
- Establish reassuring rules of conduct.
- Be consistent in enforcing the rules of conduct.
- Impose logical consequences when children disobey the rules of conduct.
- Reduce children's stress as much as possible by preparing them for change.
- Provide children with ways of reducing their stress by introducing relaxing activities.

Did you know?

Between 9 and 12 months, children start to recognize themselves in the mirror. Between 15 and 18 months they can distinguish other people in photos and around 20 months, they can identify themselves as a girl or boy. Around the age of 3, they begin to use the pronoun "me" in speaking of themselves. In discovering themselves, children also discover that they have less need of others. They develop a distance from others, which continues evolving as they grow.

Fostering self-knowledge

Why is self-knowledge important?

Self-knowledge is a necessary prerequisite for self-esteem. Learning to know oneself is a process that lasts a lifetime. Self-knowledge becomes increasingly precise as we go through life, and acts as a kind of pillar for self-esteem. Whether we are children, teenagers or adults, we must have knowledge of ourselves before we can acknowledge ourselves (self-esteem).

Having healthy self-esteem first means knowing ourselves well enough to be able to mobilize our personal strengths while maintaining a fairly accurate view of our limitations. It is a question of confronting life's difficulties while firmly believing in ourselves, without illusions, and without any sense of having to be "the best".

How does self-knowledge develop?

Self-knowledge develops in children through their interactions with others. It is in the presence of people important to them that children perform the many physical, social and intellectual activities that help them develop their skills, of which they become increasingly aware.

Through learning and the reactions of the people around them, children develop knowledge of their environment and themselves. Over the course of their experiences, they become aware of their physical characteristics, needs and feelings, as well as their physical, intellectual and social skills.

No matter what age they are, every time children learn something they sever a bond of dependence, progressively growing away from the people around them. Self-knowledge and the certainty of being a full-fledged person are things that evolve over time.

One-of-a-kind or like everyone else?

All children possess distinctive characteristics from the time they are born. They have their own personality, express needs differently and develop at their own pace. Through their actions, reactions, needs and feelings, children demonstrate that they are different from their parents and other children.

It is by noticing that they are different from others that children become aware of who they are, and develop a sense of personal identity. If we felt identical to someone else in every way, we could not become aware of our own identity. That is why children have to understand what sets them apart from other people.

Children must become aware that they do not have the same type of face or physical build as other people; they possess a unique set of skills, physical, intellectual and social; they possess character traits shared by no one around them. These differences, which children discover over time, help them see themselves as individuals, "one-of-a-kind".

In their quest for identity, children also perceive that they possess the same skills as other children, or react in the same way, or have similar personality traits. In this balancing of differences and similarities, children acquire a sound knowledge of themselves.

Can adult expectations be harmful?

It is completely normal to have expectations of one's children, but it is important that these be realistic. Parents whose expectations are too specific are in danger of being disappointed, of focusing more attention on their children's weak points and negative characteristics.

Adults, parents and teachers, have many expectations of children. Why do we attach so much importance to performance, results and exploits? Why do we follow children's development with a magnifying glass? Could this reflect our own desire to achieve total success through them? This attitude is devastating for children; though they resemble us, they are also very different from us.

Children want more than anything to be loved and will go to great lengths to achieve this goal. They may even go against their own fundamental nature. Children who are never satisfied with themselves, who criticize themselves, destroy their drawings and panic if they don't get the highest marks at school, are convinced they cannot be loved unless they are perfect. They believe they are always falling short of expectations, and may develop symptoms related to performance anxiety (nausea, stomachaches, insomnia, etc.), as well as feelings of depression – and this can occur even if parents have not openly expressed their expectations.

Too many parents and teachers, uncompromising perfectionists with themselves and others, tend to fixate on children's imperfections and forget their strengths and qualities. In bringing up children, we have to give up perfectionism, forget about the dream child to discover the real child. It is important to have expectations of children, but these should reflect the children's own interests, abilities and pace of development.

Stephen, or behavioural difficulties

On the school's recommendation, a mother asks for help for her son Stephen, who displays pronounced behavioural difficulties in class and at home. Stephen is in third grade and displays no learning disabilities. His performance at school has always been above average. However, his teacher can no longer cope with his aggressive, even violent behaviour. Stephen throws tantrums two or three times a day, when the teacher is giving him instructions or simply when he is frustrated. At home, too, he has a very low tolerance for frustration. His anger builds and he often loses control of himself. He yells, throws things, and sometimes even hits other children. At home he uses foul language with his mother, and sometimes kicks and punches her.

Stephen lives alone with his mother and rarely sees his father. His parents separated when he was 4 years old. He witnessed domestic violence prior to the father's departure. The mother works full-time in a factory and emphasizes that she is very tired in the evening. She feels guilty for not being able to spend more time with her child. However, she does activities with her son and takes him on outings over the weekend. She judges herself a bad mother, and feels overwhelmed by Stephen's behaviour. She even says that she should never have become a mother.

When Stephen has calmed down from his tantrums he says he is "bad". His mother sometimes compares him to his father, saying that he is violent " just like him". She tells him often, after one of his fits of anger, that he is uncontrollable, bad. Stephen recognizes none of his own good qualities or skills.

At school, his behaviour, which has always been hard to manage, has become even more so in recent months. His teacher makes efforts to encourage him, without much success. In fact, she no longer dares to compliment him because his behaviour becomes even more difficult when she does.

Intervention

Stephen sees himself in a very negative light. This view is fed by the negative judgments of his mother and the people at school. The child tends to repeat the violent gestures he witnessed between his father and mother, as a result of intergenerational transmission. Displaying violence, Stephen confirms his negative self-image, an image also confirmed by the negative judgments of adults. He is more and more convinced that he is "bad". He is in the process of internalizing a negative identity that he seeks unconsciously to maintain through the compulsive repetition of violent gestures. Unconsciously, he defends his negative identity by adopting even more difficult behaviour when he is praised. Stephen must be helped to curb this process of self-depreciation and negative identity by developing in him a sense of self-worth. This cannot happen without a battle between the "good" and "bad" Stephen. Adults have to become the allies of the good Stephen, who does exist, in spite of appearances. Here are the strategies that were suggested and applied:

- Re-validation of the mother's parental competency. She is not aware that she displays parenting skills in showing warmth towards

Stephen, making sure he is well-dressed and well-fed, and making an effort to do constructive activities with him over the weekend.

- Providing time off for the mother, with the help of community services, so she can rest, meet and exchange with other parents who are experiencing difficulties.
- Helping the mother be respected by Stephen by suggesting that she establish a few rules, which must always be clear, and most of all, consistent.
- Adults must bring Stephen to understand that it is his violent gestures that they find unacceptable, not Stephen himself.
- In the evening, after tucking him into bed, remind him of two or three positive actions he performed during the day.
- Help Stephen become aware that he finds it hard to accept praise because it contradicts his negative view of himself.
- Help Stephen become aware of his good qualities and skills by reminding him of positive acts that he cannot deny.
- Help him become aware of his progress by concretely emphasizing his small accomplishments.

What are the signs of good self-knowledge in children?

Young children cannot be expected to acquire a great deal of self-knowledge or develop a complete sense of their own identity. That is the work of a lifetime! However, occasionally and in different ways, children may adopt the following attitudes and behaviours:

- they are able to recognize their physical skill, or lack thereof;
- they are able to recognize their intellectual skill, or lack thereof;
- they are able to recognize their interpersonal skills, or lack thereof;
- they are able to recognize their creative skill, or lack thereof;
- they are able to see what makes them different from others;
- they are able to assert themselves;
- they are able to discern the actions and words other people appreciate in them;
- they are able to make choices;
- they are able to express preferences and ideas;
- they are able to express feelings;
- they are capable of building an awareness of the connection between their needs, feelings and behaviour;
- they are able to express needs;
- they are able to inspire respect;

- they are able to take on age-appropriate responsibilities;
- they are able to remember past accomplishments.

What are the parental attitudes that are most harmful to children's self-esteem?

A "negative" upbringing. The upbringing of most adults today was based on pinpointing their mistakes and shortcomings. This upbringing was largely conditioned by negative messages that often prevented parents from seeing the good side of children and emphasizing their positive acts. This kind of upbringing gave adults deeply ingrained reflexes that are revealed in remarks such as: "He doesn't know his alphabet though he's been repeating it for months," "She never cleans up her room". When adults describe children's behaviour with words like 'always' and 'never', it makes them feel helpless and prevents them from changing.

Words that hurt. Some words are like caresses, but others are deeply wounding. That is why it is very important to address children in a respectful manner. To develop self-respect, they must feel respected by others. Little nicknames with negative connotations, even when spoken in a non-aggressive manner, end up giving children a sense that they have less value than others. Negative and frequent criticism, sharp remarks, scathing judgments all deal terrible blows to children's self-esteem

What are the parental attitudes that promote self-knowledge in children?

Parents should adopt attitudes and methods of promoting self-knowledge in their children. They should try to:

- build a close and loving relationship with their children;
- recognise and accept the differences between their own children and other children;
- give up the dream child;
- set realistic goals for learning and behaviour;
- demonstrate empathy and warmth;
- speak to their children respectfully;
- avoid labelling children with words like "lazy", "slow", etc. ;
- focus on their children's strengths, good qualities and skills;
- give positive feedback regularly;

Did you know?

- Accepting children as they are is to treat them with dignity.
- It is very important for children to be taken seriously.
- Children's self-esteem is gravely harmed by the unrealistic expectations of parents and other adults around them!

- help children become aware that they are unique because of their physical characteristics, personal qualities and special skills;
- encourage assertiveness and independence;
- help children become aware of their needs and express them appropriately;
- help children understand that there is a connection between their needs, feelings and behaviours;
- pay attention to the difficulties children encounter and help them to overcome them;
- avoid pointing out unacceptable behaviour in front of others;
- blame the unacceptable behaviour, not the child.

It would be unrealistic to expect parents to adopt all these attitudes, or use every one of these guidelines all the time. However, it is important for them to regularly examine the quality of their relationship with their children. Children's self-esteem is profoundly affected by their interpersonal environment.

DUBLIN

Fostering a sense of belonging

‣ Is it important to belong to a group and have relationships with others?

Human beings cannot live in complete independence from other people, isolated and withdrawn. Humans are social beings by nature. They need to belong to a group, to be connected to others and feel they are part of a social network. Children are no exception, and their need to be part of a group becomes stronger as they grow older.

We all need recognition from others in order to exist. Children need to be seen by their parents; teachers wouldn't exist without their students; friends compare themselves to each other. Whether we want to be seen as similar to others or different from them, they are the ones who confirm our existence.

These days, children spend a lot of time in organized groups (day-care, school, recreational activities, etc.) that play an important role in their development. These groups are necessary because they give children a chance to expand their horizons, adapt to group dynamics that are not those of the family, and by extension, adapt to society in general.

▸ What is meant by "social self-esteem"?

The human being needs to belong to a group, feel connected to a social network, and most of all have a close companion, as well as friends. Sharing stories, doing things with others, laughing, singing, all these things make us feel whole and happy. In times of difficulty, friends are on our side and protect us from solitude. To be loved and appreciated helps us confront many situations. The things others say, the way they look at us and listen to us, in short, the way they view us, all help us define ourselves and make us want to be better. The feeling of belonging is an antidote to social isolation.

Social self-esteem, or the self-worth we derive from social interaction, is developed through the process of socialization and is reinforced by our belonging to a group. Am I important to others? Are they important to me? How much do I value myself in relation to my family, my group of friends, my colleagues at work? All these questions are related to social self-esteem. People who feel that their presence in a group is unimportant and has no effect on the group, in fact believe that they are of little value to others. They probably feel very lonely and need to work on their social self-esteem in order to experience a feeling of belonging.

▸ How do children learn socialization skills?

In the first years of life, children have a very close relationship with their parents, which serves as the basis of self-esteem. From the age of 2, children love being with other small children; even if they cannot really play with other children, they love their company. At this age, they are aware of other children, observing and imitating them. They are more or less solitary, playing in the others' presence and gradually learning to tolerate their proximity. Children of this age are especially interested in the others' games and... their toys. Their language is not yet sufficiently developed for them to ask another child to give them the object that they would like to play with. At this stage of life, one frequently observes conflicts over the sharing of toys.

At around 4, children become very vocal about wanting to be with friends. Even the most patient and available parent cannot be the wonderful friend that another child be. Hair pulling, toy grabbing, learning to negotiate and share are all part of social education. At this age, children mostly play matching or cooperative games, which involve parallel operations within the same activity. Children may well be interested in joining a group at play, but are clumsy in their way of showing it. At this age, what counts most for children are shared preferences. Playmates change often, according to the interest that is shared.

Thus throughout a child's development, we observe a decline in parental influence and a rise in the influence of friends. Little by little, children grow away from their parents to discover the social dimension.

From 5 to 12, in the primary school period, the majority of children are visibly motivated by many of the same factors:

- the desire to be loved, valued and accepted by others, especially by those of the same age and sex;
- the tendency to imitate others, especially people the children admire and value;

- the desire to resemble those they love and respect;
- the desire to avoid rejection at all costs.

Children feel a strong desire to belong to a group of friends. Gradually, their emotional dependence on adults declines and social dependence on friends increases. Through their relationships with friends, children come to feel valued by others.

Where do children really learn to develop their social skills?

It is in the **family** that children are initiated into life in society. The family is the first group to which children belong, and family-life greatly conditions and influences their future ability to adapt. Once in **school**, children want to expand their circle of friends and be accepted by a greater number of people. They want to learn to adapt to others and be more like them. They first learn **to enter into contact** with others without forcing themselves upon them, **to assert** themselves in a constructive manner (say who they are and how they are different, express likes and dislikes...), **consider** the opinions and needs of others, control their words and gestures (**self-control**), and **resolve conflicts**.

The feeling of belonging to a school is fundamental. School becomes a place of choice for furthering the development of children's socialisation and building a feeling of belonging. At school, children learn to make a place for themselves in a group. They learn to make friends, adapt to rules, to win and lose, to talk and assert themselves, as well as take on responsibilities. They also learn to socialize their urges and put their special skills at the service of a larger community.

What are the signs of a sense of belonging in children?

Children with a strong sense of belonging to a group display most of the following attitudes and behaviours:

- they actively seek out others;
- they are relaxed in a group;
- they find it easy to communicate with others;
- they find it easy to remember group cheers, songs, etc.;
- they are sensitive to others;
- they are capable of generosity;
- they are capable of sharing and helping other people;
- they sometimes suggest ideas that could be useful to the group;
- they take on small responsibilities within the group;
- they talk about their friends or the group at home;
- they are capable of applying strategies to resolve social problems.

What are the parental attitudes that promote a sense of belonging?

- Being a model of sensitivity, sharing and generosity to others.
- Planning activities that will give pleasure to the entire family.
- Promoting justice and equality in the family.
- Cultivating a sense of pride in belonging to the family.

- Giving children little responsibilities and praising them for contributing to family life.
- Promoting a climate of respect among family members.
- Encouraging children to be sensitive to the social dimension.
- Encouraging children to be generous, to share and help others.
- Inviting your children's friends to your home.
- Suggesting strategies for resolving social problems.
- Giving positive feedback on social skills.
- Volunteering to help with different activities in the day-care and at school.

Did you know?

- All discipline is based on a loving relationship.
- Rules are necessary for the smooth functioning of all social groups, including the family.
- Children and teenagers need to find their place in a group of friends.
- A successful social life acts as a defence against depression.
- Good communication stems from two basic attitudes: sincere interest in what other people say, without judgment, criticism or argument, and with frankness.
- Enjoyment at play, enjoyment in learning, enjoyment in living in society are all important for the building of healthy self-esteem.

Fostering a sense of competency

▸ Where do children acquire their knowledge?

It is not at school that people acquire the greater part of their knowledge. The great American teacher Benjamin Bloom demonstrated that we acquire 80% of our knowledge outside of school. When children enter nursery school, they have already acquired a great deal of knowledge, mostly from their parents. They have a grasp of complex skills such as speaking, which is learned simply through the close relationship of children and parents. This relationship is the very essence of children's self-esteem. When they perceive that they are truly loved, they conclude that they are loveable and therefore valuable.

▸ What is meant by "a sense of competency"?

A sense of competency is defined as the internalizing and recording of memories of personal successes and goal-achievement in different areas of life. This feeling displays itself in a deep-seated motivation to pursue goals, a private conviction that one can rise to challenges and acquire different kinds of knowledge. A sense of competency is not something that happens by magic. It develops over years and numerous experiences of goals successfully attained.

What steps do children go through to acquire a sense of competency?

There are two stages that precede the lasting appearance of a true sense of competency. Before 7 or 8 years, children experience success by focusing on results and final products. That means that they are concentrating on only one thing at a time: the action they are performing for the simple pleasure of doing it, or the result of that action. Their thinking is not sufficiently developed to co-ordinate actions and results in a logical manner; consequently, they perceive few causal relationships between their attitudes, strategies (or ways of doing things) and the result obtained. However, their successes gradually increase their motivation to undertake new projects if the adults around them make them conscious of their accomplishments. When adults talk to children about their successes, children become aware that they are performing positive actions, which helps motivate them to take on new challenges.

After experiencing the feeling of success based on final results, children must experience a feeling of efficiency, the other prerequisite stage in acquiring a sense of competency. A feeling of efficiency is the sense of self-worth that results from an accurate understanding of how attitudes and strategies are linked to the successful achievement of a result. Children experience a feeling of efficiency when they become aware that results are not obtained by magic, but as the logical consequence of a procedure.

The logical equation of learning is as follows:

ATTITUDES
(attention, motivation, independence, responsibility)
+
STRATEGIES
(ways or means of doing things)
=
RESULTS
(success or failure in achieving a goal)

Valerie, or learning difficulties

Parents request help for their daughter Valerie, who is experiencing learning difficulties and failure in mathematics. Valerie is in Grade 4 and her academic performance has been weak in math since Grade 2. However, she has always been competent in English class, especially in reading. Her parents do not understand the reasons for this disparity.

Valerie loves reading. When she's reading, images come readily to her mind, and she demonstrates strong logical ability in reading comprehension. However, her logical reasoning skills do not extend to mathematics. She is incapable of learning the multiplication tables, and when she has to solve math problems she feels defeated even before she begins, convinced she will fail. She displays anxiety while doing her math homework, especially before tests. This anxiety, sometimes dramatic, prevents her from mobilizing her skills for abstract thinking and logical reasoning.

In short, Valerie displays a rich imagination in her games at home and written compositions, and is aware of her ability and success in English class, but belittles herself about her performance in math, calling herself "stupid" and "dummy."

Intervention

Valerie is caught in a vicious circle. Her anxiety predisposes her to failure, which in turn increases her anxiety. Her parents, school personnel and specialists must help Valerie to defuse her negative image of mathematics and be more confident about the subject. Here are the strategies that were suggested and applied to help develop Valerie's sense of competency about mathematics.

- Help Valerie become aware that she shows good ability for abstract thinking and logical reasoning in reading comprehension, and that these skills can be applied to mathematics.
- Help her solve problems requiring logic and deduction without mathematical operations.
- Help her use her reading comprehension skills to better understand math problems.

Make her aware of her skills and successes while working on these math problems.

- Start an Achievement Diary in which she writes down all her accomplishments at school, including those in mathematics.
- Before a math exam, encourage her to read her Achievement Diary to put her back in touch with her skills.
- Make her aware of the inhibiting effects of her anxiety about mathematics. Help her reduce her anxiety by taking deep breaths, using relaxation techniques, recalling past successes and using sound work strategies.
- Guide her parents towards attributing less value to marks and more value to Valerie's learning process and strategies.

▸ What is the role of motivation?

Motivation – the thing that prompts a person to accomplish a task, or attain an objective corresponding to a need – is made up of desire and determination. It is a set of forces that compel a person to act. One could also describe motivation as an anticipation of the pleasure or usefulness of a task to be performed.

As far as academic motivation is concerned, we might say that it begins well before children enter school. In fact, the motivation to engage in intellectual activities first begins in the family. We know that before the age of 6, children tend to behave in a primarily verbal/motor fashion. However, they are intrigued when they see their parents doing something they do not do themselves, for example, holding a book or a magazine for minutes at a time. They wonder what could possibly be so interesting about this object that you can't even play with! Their increasing curiosity about adult secrets and activities is the source of their motivation to read, among other things.

If parents rarely read, have no intellectual life and take little interest in their children's schooling, there is a good chance the children will adopt the same attitude. Motivation is cultivated - it cannot be forced. However, parents can play a supportive role in this regard. To understand the parents' role, we need only to compare motivation to appetite; you cannot force children to have an appetite, but you can encourage them to eat by creating varied menus and introducing appealing little dishes. Similarly, we cannot force children to learn, but we can awaken in them a desire to learn.

Does the usefulness of knowledge help motivate children?

Like adults, children are not motivated to perform tasks if they do not see their utility. Parents have an important role to play in this regard. Children should be guided to make connections between what they learn in school and the application of this knowledge in everyday life. This kind of guidance helps nurture children's motivation and prompts them to use their knowledge in a variety of situations.

Independence or overprotection?

Independence is generally defined as a person's ability to be free and independent, from a moral and intellectual point of view, and base his or her behaviour on freely-chosen rules and values. It essentially consists of the ability to break the ties of dependence on the people around us and make our own choices.

Overprotection, on the other hand, is an attitude that is very harmful to independence. Overprotecting children means doing something in their place, even though they are quite capable of doing it themselves. This kind of attitude impedes the development of independence in children, especially if they are exposed to it on a regular basis. Overprotection keeps children dependent, and their self-esteem is affected; in fact, when parents do something in their children's place, they are sending the message that the children are incapable of doing it themselves. They are conveying a judgment of incompetence.

What are the signs of a sense of competency in children?

Children who possess a solid sense of competency display most of the following attitudes and behaviours:

- they remember past successes;
- they anticipate enjoyment of an activity;

Did you know?

Working to develop children's self-esteem means being engaged in an educational process that allows children to experience and express the best of themselves. Imagine how tomorrow's world will be if our children, as adults, lead their lives in a spirit of respect for themselves and others, viewing nature and humanity as an inseparable whole which must be cared for!

Did you know?

- We cannot want on our children's behalf.
- Children, like adults, react to stress with physical symptoms (headaches, stomach aches, nervous tics...), with behavioural or learning problems (aggressiveness, withdrawal, memory loss...).
- To encourage our children - honestly, without idle flattery - is to give them hope in the future.

- they understand the importance of suggested activities or learning;
- they feel proud when they succeed;
- they want to learn;
- they demonstrate intellectual curiosity;
- they are able to choose between different strategies and methods;
- they persevere despite difficulties;
- they show creativity;
- they take initiative and calculated risks;
- they are able to re-apply and generalize skills and knowledge;
- they acknowledge and accept errors;
- they remain relaxed while learning.

▸ What are the parental attitudes that promote a sense of competency?

There is a wide range of attitudes that parents can adopt to foster a sense of competency in their children:

- understand their children's abilities and level of development;
- help children remember past successes;
- suggest stimulating, enjoyable activities;
- tell their children about the usefulness of activities and learning;
- suggest realistic goals that match their children's abilities;
- foster their children's independence;

- encourage a sense of responsibility in their children;
- regularly review goals and give feedback to help children understand the connection between their attitudes, strategies and results;
- suggest different strategies and ways of learning;
- help children recognize, minimize and accept mistakes;
- help children correct their mistakes;
- encourage their children's creativity;
- help children avoid performance anxiety;
- emphasize the importance of learning;
- emphasize children's effective strategies and responses with positive feedback;
- respect children's individual pace of learning;
- stimulate children's thought development.

Are parents' and teachers' expectations sometimes too extreme?

It is normal to have expectations of children to prevent them from growing passive, dependent and self-demeaning. For example, if parents display indifference as to whether their children learn or not, if they do not encourage them to go after challenges, they appear incompetent. But if they do have expectations, these must be realistic, that is, adapted to children's development and individual pace of learning. If the adult's ambitions are too great, children may experience performance-related stress, as well as failures that damage their self-esteem.

Therefore, the learning challenges that we suggest to children must match their abilities; they must be adapted to their level and pace of development. Children who fail because the fixed objective is too high or because the learning pace is too accelerated, will experience no enjoyment. Instead, their motivation will suffer and they will feel badly about themselves.

Everything depends on the setting of appropriate objectives. When goals are matched to children's abilities, and children use good strategies, they can surmount obstacles, learn new things and achieve a sense of efficiency and self-worth. On the other hand, if children are presented with activities that are too easy and repetitive, they simply feel boredom and diminished self-esteem, for they deduce that people have judged them not sufficiently competent to perform more difficult tasks. Indeed, when we set goals for children that are too complex and beyond their level of skill, they experience a sense of failure and depreciation, resulting in a decrease in their level of self-esteem.

Being a competent parent

▸ What is meant by "a sense of parental competency"?

A parent's role is rich and complex. According to popular opinion, parents are capable of having good relationships with their children, responding to their needs and fostering their development in the appropriate conditions. But in order to adequately respond to children's needs and pace of development, parents must have acquired certain attitudes and skills. Thus we define parental competency in terms of parents' concrete ability to respond to their children's needs and transmit their own values.

However, a distinction must be made between parental competency, as such, and a sense of competency, that is, the parents' internalized view of their competency as parents. On this subject, we may mention that some parents adopt attitudes and educational strategies that are well adapted to their children's needs, yet, in spite of everything, still judge themselves as lacking competency. In the case of such parents, we might wonder if they are not overly demanding of themselves and in fact, underestimate their competency. Then there are parents who, perhaps in order to "look good", overestimate their parenting skills when in truth, their attitudes are not at all attuned to their children's needs.

Certain prerequisites are essential to the achievement of parental competency: emotional maturity, good intellectual functioning and realistic expectations of their role as parents. Parents who are immature, overly-focused on their own needs or who have not learned to control their impulses, will certainly have trouble empathizing with their children and recognizing their needs. Parents who are too rigid, or have a limited capacity for self-questioning, experience great difficulty in adapting to new experiences and adjusting their attitudes accordingly. Finally, parents with an overly idyllic image of childhood and overly high expectations of their children are liable to experience failure and disappointment as parents.

A sense of parental competency, as well as true competency, is based on two fundamental attitudes: the capacity for closeness, and empathy. Closeness between parents and children creates bonds that are indelible, visceral and unconditional. Empathy is also essential if parents are to respond appropriately to their children's needs, and acquire a sense of parental competency. It is also important for parents to be truly available to children, and remove the focus from themselves in order to "read" and understand their children's needs. Hence, closeness between parents and children, and empathy in relation to children's needs, are essential to good child development.

What are the qualities of a competent parent?

Here are the main qualities of competent parents, that is, parents who capably guide their children's development. These parents:

- adopt a healthy lifestyle;
- respond to their children's needs;
- ensure the child's physical safety;
- by being present, ensure children stability in space and time;
- are available to their children;
- show empathy for their children;
- foster a reassuring bond with children;
- stimulate their children at different levels: physical, sensorial, intellectual, social and moral;
- respect the pace of their children's development;
- are open to communicating with their children;
- most of the time, take account of their children's ideas and opinions;
- propose alternatives to their children;
- establish clear boundaries;
- make decisions without ambivalence about their values;
- actively embody the values they believe in;
- are able to be firm on some issues and flexible on others;
- help children take on responsibility;
- avoid power struggles;
- encourage children's curiosity;
- encourage children's social life.

Parents who recognize most of these characteristics in themselves are justified in feeling they possess a good sense of parental competency.

Is self-esteem the solution to every problem?

Self-esteem is not only a matter of knowing our strengths and skills. It also involves having an accurate perception of our limitations. Thus it is important for adults to help children become aware of their difficulties, representing them as challenges that their children are able to overcome.

But we must not believe that self-esteem is the solution to every problem. We must resist the kind of magical thinking that represents self-esteem as the key to all behaviours; we should be wary of the popular opinion that if only people acquired better self-esteem, the world would be a better place.

Nonetheless, to believe in the importance of self-esteem is to have confidence in human beings and their ability to evolve, even in the worst conditions.

Did you know?

There are six key words for the development of self-esteem in children and teens: pleasure, love, security, independence, pride, hope.

Self-esteem is the most valuable gift that parents can give their children. This gift can only be transmitted through close relationships and loving attitudes. Children who are physically and psychologically secure, who feel confident about life, who know themselves and their own identities, who have a strong sense of belonging to their family and a group, who develop their skills and are aware of their own value, have received a great gift they may rely on in times of difficulty. This gift is a passport to ongoing growth and development, the best passport that a child can possess.

To learn more about child's self-esteem

Freeing Your Child from Negative Thinking: Powerful, Practical Strategies to Build a Lifetime of Resilience, Flexibility, and Happiness. *Tamar E. Chansky*. Cambridge, MA., Da Capo Press, 2008. 321 p.

Helping Children to Build Self-Esteem: a Photocopiable Activities Book. *Deborah M. Plummer*. London, Eng.: Jessica Kingsley, 2007. 285 p.

Raising Your Child's Inner Self-Esteem: the Authoritative Guide from Infancy through the Teen Years. *Karen Owens*. Cambridge, MA : Da Capo Press, 2003. 355 p.

Self-Esteem: A Passport for Life. *Germain Duclos*. Montreal: Editions du CHU Sainte-Justine, 2001. 114 p.

501 Tips to Boost Your Child's Self-Esteem. *Robert D. Ramsey*. Toronto: McGrawHill Co., 2nd ed., 2003. 240 p.

The children

Antoine Dolbec Leclerc, cover
Félix Leclerc-Lamontagne, page 2
Olivia et Béatrice Ma, page 8
Julien, Laurent et Philippe St-Vil, page 17
Sophie Alchourron, page 18
Emmanuel Lavoie, page 22
Zoé Blanchette, page 30
Trisan Bilodeau, page 42
Marie Dewolf, page 51
Sébastien Lavoie, page 55

In the same collection

What Should I Know about my Child's Sexuality?
Frédérique Saint-Pierre, Marie-France Viau

What Should I Know about my Child's Development?
Francine Ferland

What Should I Know about my Teen?
Céline Boisvert